Growing Readers

Memorial Day

by Helen Frost

Consulting Editor: Gail Saunders-Smith, Ph.D.
Consultant: Alexa Sandmann, Ed.D.
Professor of Literacy
The University of Toledo
Member, National Council for the Social Studies

Pebble Books

an imprint of Capstone Press
Mankato, Minnesota

Pebble Books are published by Capstone Press
151 Good Counsel Drive, P.O. Box 669, Mankato, Minnesota 56002
http://www.capstone-press.com

2 3 4 5 6 05 04 03 02 01

Library of Congress Cataloging-in-Publication Data
Frost, Helen, 1949–
     Memorial Day/by Helen Frost.
     p. cm.—(National holidays)
     Includes bibliographical references and index.
     Summary: Explains how and why Memorial Day came to be celebrated as
a holiday.
     ISBN 0-7368-0544-3
     1. Memorial Day—Juvenile literature. [1. Memorial Day. 2. Holidays.] I. Title.
II. Series.
E642.F74 2000
394.262—dc21   99-052876

Note to Parents and Teachers

The National Holidays series supports national social studies
standards related to understanding events that celebrate the values
and principles of American democracy. This book describes and
illustrates Memorial Day. The photographs support early readers
in understanding the text. This book also introduces early readers to
subject-specific vocabulary words, which are defined in the Words
to Know section. Early readers may need assistance to read some
words and to use the Table of Contents, Words to Know, Read
More, Internet Sites, and Index/Word List sections of the book.

Table of Contents

Memorial Day is a national holiday in the United States. Americans celebrate Memorial Day on the last Monday of May.

6

Memorial Day began soon after the Civil War ended in 1865. The Northern states and the Southern states fought the Civil War.

Many people died in the Civil War. Some states honored these people on a special day.

This day sometimes was called Decoration Day. People decorated soldiers' graves with wreaths and flags.

Many U.S. soldiers
died in other wars too.
Now Memorial Day is
a time to remember all
of these soldiers.

HONORING
WOMEN
WHO SERVED

14

People have parades on Memorial Day. They fly flags at half-mast to show respect.

People throw flowers on water. Flowers honor soldiers who died at sea.

Families gather on Memorial Day. They talk about family members who have died.

Students talk about war. They learn about peace and freedom.

⭐ Words to Know

Civil War—the U.S. war between the Northern states and the Southern states; the Civil War lasted from 1861 to 1865.

decorate—to add items to make something look nice; people decorate graves and statues with flowers, wreaths, and flags on Memorial Day.

half-mast—the place halfway between the top and the bottom of a flagpole; people fly flags at half-mast to show respect for someone who has died.

Memorial Day—a national holiday celebrated in the United States on the last Monday of May; Memorial Day honors Americans who have died in wars.

national—having to do with a country as a whole; Memorial Day is a holiday for the whole country.

soldier—someone who is in the military

Read More

Ansary, Mir Tamim. *Memorial Day.* Holiday Histories. Des Plaines, Ill.: Heinemann Library, 1999.

Barkin, Carol and Elizabeth James. *The Holiday Handbook.* New York: Clarion Books, 1994.

Sorensen, Lynda. *Memorial Day.* Holidays. Vero Beach, Fla.: Rourke, 1994.

Internet Sites

Memorial Day
http://usmemorialday.org

Memorial Day
http://wilstar.com/holidays/memday.htm

Memorial Day
http://www.dcn.davis.ca.us/vme/memorial

Memorial Day
http://www.rootsweb.com/~nyseneca/memorial.htm

Index/Word List

Word Count: 142
Early-Intervention Level: 17

Editorial Credits
Mari C. Schuh, editor; Heather Kindseth, cover designer; Linda Clavel, illustrator; Kimberly Danger, photo researcher

Photo Credits
Archive Photos, 6
Colephoto/Robin Cole, 12
David F. Clobes, 16, 20
Index Stock Imagery/Rudi Von Briel, 4
No Greater Love, 10
Photri-Microstock, 8, 14 (bottom)
Unicorn Stock Photos/Jean Higgins, cover; Chromosohm and Sohm, 1
Uniphoto/David Stover, 18
Richard B. Levine, 14 (top)